DRUGS AND YOUR PARENTS

It is lonely being the child of a chemically dependent parent.

THE DRUG ABUSE PREVENTION LIBRARY

DRUGS AND YOUR PARENTS

Rhoda McFarland

THE ROSEN PUBLISHING GROUP, INC.
NEW YORK

Published in 1991 by The Rosen Publishing Group, Inc.
29 East 21st Street, New York, NY 10010

First Edition

Manufactured in the United States of America.

Library of Congress Cataloging-in-Publication Data

McFarland, Rhoda
    Drugs and your parents/Rhoda McFarland—1st ed.
    (The Drug Abuse Prevention Library)
    Includes bibliographical references and index.
    Summary: Readers who have a parent or parents that are
    alcohol/drug abusers learn how to survive in a chemically
    dependent household, and find out where to get help for
    their parent(s) and themselves.
        ISBN 0-8239-1261-2
        1. Children of alcoholics—Juvenile literature.
        2. Children of narcotic addicts—Juvenile litera-
    ture. 3. Parent and teenager—Juvenile literature.
    [1. Alcoholism. 2. Drug abuse. 3. Parent and
    child.] I. Title. II. Series.
    HV5066.M35 1991
    362.29'13—dc20   91-9188
                                             CIP
                                            AC

Contents

Introduction

*A*s used in this book, the word "drug" means *any* mood-changing chemical. This includes alcohol.

The term "chemical dependence" is used in place of "alcoholism" and "drug addiction" many times in the book. No difference is made between alcohol and other drugs. Whatever the drug, its effect is the same on people. People like you and me.

Being the child of an alcoholic or addict is often very lonely. You may think you're the only one who feels the way you do. You may think that no one understands. There *are* people who understand and care. There are millions of teens just like you. There are millions who are no longer teens who are just like you, too. Many have worked or are working hard to over-come the effects of living with a chemically dependent parent. Because they know the pain of alcoholism or addiction, they're willing to help you. You need only ask for help. Read on to learn how to do that.

Fact Sheet

- Twenty million young people under eighteen live with one or two alcoholic parents.
- In a classroom of twenty-five, there are four to six with alcoholic parents.
- Forty to sixty percent of children with chemically dependent parents become chemically dependent themselves.
- Children of alcoholics/addicts have more problems with alcohol and other drugs than children from homes with no chemically dependent family members.
- Twenty percent of caseloads of juvenile courts and child guidance clinics are children from alcoholic homes.
- Forty to sixty percent of all child abuse is related to alcohol and other drugs.
- Eighty percent of family violence is drug-related.

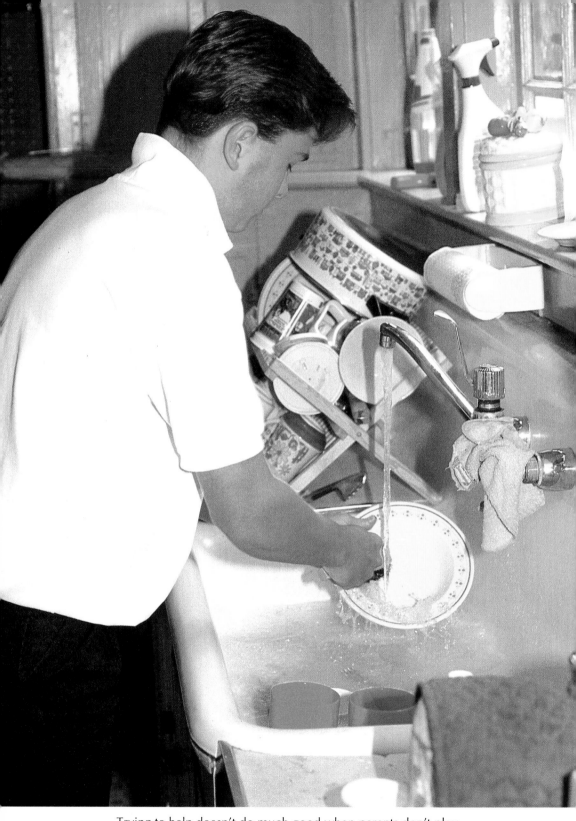

Trying to help doesn't do much good when parents don't play their part.

CHAPTER 1

What's Wrong with Them Anyway?

"How could he do it after he promised?" Kathy stared straight ahead and didn't look at anyone. She was so embarrassed and angry. Her father had promised not to drink before he came to the game. It was the last game, and the team could win the title. He hadn't come to one game all season. He told her he would be here tonight, and he *promised* not to drink. Everybody could see that he was drunk. Kathy wished she could disappear.

Gary knew that his parents smoked pot. All their friends did, too. But this was something else. He asked his mother for money for lunch. She told him to get it out of her purse. When he took out her wallet, he saw a little glass bottle with

10 white stuff in it. A small spoon was attached to the bottle. Gary had seen pictures of cocaine. How could his parents mess around with cocaine?

Kathy and Gary are two of over twenty million Americans under eighteen whose parents abuse *drugs*. "How could they?" these young people ask again and again. "Why can't she see what she's doing?" "Why does he act like that?" "What's wrong with them anyway?"

What's wrong is *chemical dependence*. It does not matter whether the chemical is alcohol, cocaine, or another drug; the effect is the same. Addiction to alcohol (*alcoholism*) or to other drugs is a disease. The people who have the disease don't know it and won't admit it. They blame others for their problems. That is *denial*. Denial is one of the signs of the disease.

People with the disease of chemical dependence change from glad to mad in a flash. Their behavior is often embarrassing and improper. They have a *compulsion* to use chemicals. They must do it again and again. When they they drink or use, they lose control over how much they use and how long they use. We call that *addiction*. That's why Kathy's father didn't keep his promise not to drink. He didn't mean to get drunk. He was just going to have one drink before he went to the game. Once he started drinking, he couldn't stop. He didn't want to drink. He had to. He can't control his drinking. It controls him. He doesn't drink to feel good. He drinks to feel less bad. Kathy's father doesn't think he has a problem. His denial is so great that he can't see how his behavior affects Kathy.

Some people think that problems cause chemical dependence. That isn't true. Chemical dependence is a *primary* disease. That means it is not caused by some other disease or problem. *It causes* problems. It leads to mental and emotional problems as well as bodily diseases.

The disease of chemical dependence is *progressive.* That means it gets worse. Gary was shocked when he found cocaine in his mother's bag. He knew his parents smoked pot. The move to cocaine is a sign that their disease is progressing. The part of their brain that makes decisions is messed up by drugs. Denial keeps them from seeing or admitting that anything is wrong.

If Kathy's father and Gary's parents get help, their disease can be stopped from getting worse.

12 Without help, chemically dependent people die sooner than people who don't use drugs. Even when they don't die from the disease itelf, their death is often caused by their drug use.

Who Becomes Chemically Dependent?

Not everyone who drinks or uses other drugs becomes chemically dependent. No one knows what causes the disease. It is known that children of alcoholics are most likely to become chemically dependent. If you have one parent who is alcoholic, you have a fifty-fifty chance of becoming chemically dependent. If both parents are chemically dependent, your chance of having the disease is even higher.

Chemical dependence runs in families. In early 1990 it was announced that an inherited *gene* carries alcoholism. Further study is being done to learn more. It is important to understand that you are at high risk for the disease if a family member is addicted to any drug.

How Can You Tell if Your Parents Are Chemically Dependent?

Your parents don't have to be drunk or high all the time to be chemically dependent. Addiction has to do with getting the

If you get rid of their supply, they know how to get more.

drug, using the drug, and trying to live a normal life. It is not how much or how often people use drugs. The important thing is what happens to them when they do. Here are questions to ask yourself:

- Do you worry about your parents' chemical use?
- Have you ever been embarrassed by it?
- Are most of your parents' friends users or heavy drinkers?
- Do you ever lie to cover up your parents' drug use?
- Have your parents ever forgotten what happened while they were drunk or high?
- Do your parents avoid parties where they can't get alcohol or other drugs?

13

14

- Do you ever feel guilty about your parents' drug use?
- Do your parents make excuses about their drug use?
- Do your parents sometimes say they are sorry after drinking or using?
- Do your parents hide chemicals around the house?
- Have you ever been afraid of what your parents might do while drunk or high?
- Have you ever been afraid to ride with your parents when they had been drinking or using?

If you answered yes to two questions, it's a sign that your parent may have a problem. Four yes answers means that there is a problem for sure. If you had more than four yes answers, the problem is serious.

What Can You Do to Make Your Parents Stop Using Chemicals?

What can you do? Remember the 3 Cs. You didn't *cause* their disease. You can't *control* it. You can't *cure* it. You *can* stop blaming yourself. You *can* stop denying and admit that there is a problem. You *can* stop covering up for your parents. You *can* find help for yourself.

CHAPTER 2

What's Going On in This House?

Sometimes Mike thought he was going crazy. Yesterday he left the wood by the door, and it was okay. Today his mother yelled at him because the wood was by the door. He never knew what would be okay from one day to the next. Michelle's father put his arm around her and called her "Princess." Ten minutes later he was shouting that she was a slob and a slut. She couldn't tell if he loved her or hated her. Yesterday Holly's mother said it was okay for Holly to go to the lake on Saturday. Today her mother got mad and said to forget about Saturday. Holly can never count on anything.

Mike's mother is an alcoholic. Michelle's father is a cocaine addict. Holly's mother is hooked on *prescription* drugs.

16 All three teenagers live with the uncertainty of chemical dependence. They never know what to expect. They can't depend on anything. Moods change in a minute. What was a happy, pleasant time is suddenly tense and unhappy.

Kathy's father promised not to drink before the game. She couldn't understand why he broke his promise.

John's father promised to go fishing with him last weekend. Instead he went to the ball game with some guys from work.

The last time Larry's mother got high on speed and was gone for three days, she promised not to do it again. She has been gone two days so far this time. Mandy's father promised to be home early. He didn't just forget her birthday dinner. He forgot to come home at all.

Broken promises break hearts. No matter how often it happens, you always hope that *this* time will be different. Maybe it has happened so many times that you don't expect anything anymore. It doesn't seem to hurt as much when you don't count on it.

Living that way creates confusion. You don't know what to do. You can't figure out what behavior is right. When promises are broken all the time you think you

You never know what to expect when a parent is out of control on drugs.

18 must be doing something wrong. There's no one to help you sort things out. Your family has the "Don't Talk" rule. You never talk to each other or anyone else about what is going on at home. You may have been told not to talk. You may be afraid that your friends won't understand. Maybe you're embarrassed and think your friends won't like you if they know what goes on in your house. You keep it all inside, and the confusion gets worse.

When Mandy's father finally came home, her mother screamed at him. They had a terrible fight. Mandy felt that it was her fault because it was her birthday dinner they were fighting about. Jeff is sixteen. He hates it when his parents fight. He's afraid that his father will kill his mother. That fear has been part of Jeff since he was a little kid with the covers over his head in the middle of the night.

A constant war goes on in chemically dependent homes. Even when your parents are not fighting, you can feel the tension. You know that a fight can break out at any time. That kind of tension makes everyone ready for a fight. Seeing parents argue and fight teaches the family how to mistreat each other. It's no wonder you fight with your brothers and sisters.

Maybe you get into arguments at school
and with your friends. That's not unusual
for young people who live in chemically
dependent homes.

Broken promises, fighting, not being
able to depend on anyone at home make
you afraid to trust others. You don't want
more disappointment. Not being able to
trust others makes you feel that you must
do everything yourself. You learn to depend on yourself. Making everything turn
out right is very important. But in your
house you can't make everything right. No
matter how hard you try, you can't please
your parent. Again, you keep it all inside.
You keep the second rule of a chemically
dependent family—"Don't trust."

Because you keep everything inside,
you think you're the only one with a family
like yours. What is going on in your house
is going on in the homes of four to six
teenagers in every classroom in your
school. They're just as confused as you
are. They don't know what is going on at
home. Most of all, they don't know what is
going on inside themselves. Like you, they
have learned the third rule in a chemically
dependent home—"Don't Feel."

Homework is even harder when parental battles are going on.

CHAPTER 3

What's Going On Inside ME?

*O*h, how she hated it when they screamed at each other. Mandy lay on the bed with her head buried in the pillow. She knew the neighbors could hear her parents fighting. It was so embarrassing. What must they think? She was so afraid that one of her friends might come by the house and hear them. She would just die if they did. She never asked anyone over because she didn't know how her father would act. When he was in a bad mood it was awful. She never knew when he might come home drunk. She didn't want people to know. They just wouldn't under-stand.

22 She's been two days this time. Larry doesn't know when his mother will be home. He's always afraid when she leaves that she won't come back. Trying to do homework is no use. He can't think about anything else. Maybe she'll be found dead somewhere. Maybe she'll take off with someone and forget all about him. Maybe she'll… Larry's mind goes crazy when his mother is gone.

The anger in his father worries Jeff. He's afraid that his father will lose control and do something terrible. When his father isn't loaded he is even worse. Jeff knows when his father is high on cocaine. When the cocaine wears off, his father gets really mean. There's a knot of worry in his stomach all the time.

Fear

Young people in chemically dependent homes live in constant fear and stress. Mandy was sure people could tell what was going on in her home. She never talked about what went on. She kept the "Don't Talk" rule. So she didn't know that Kathy, Jeff, Larry, Mike, and many others felt the same way. She didn't know she wasn't the only one.

All young people are afraid they won't be liked. Having your friends like you is very important. Most teenagers handle their fears by sharing with others. They talk to friends about their problems. They share school activities and parties. They visit each other's homes. When they are troubled they know they can get support from their family. Young people like Mandy and Larry don't have that support at home. They think something is wrong with them. They never think that something is wrong with the home. Nothing is wrong with Mandy. She deserves the support and safety that parents give. Her parents are too messed up by chemicals to give it. Because of that, Mandy thinks, "If my friends really knew me they wouldn't like me."

Fear is part of life for teenagers whose parents abuse drugs. It never goes away. Larry worries about his mother even when she's at home. The next time she can get drugs will be all it takes. He knows she will be gone again. He is afraid something will happen and she'll never come back. He hates her sometimes for using drugs and treating him badly. But he doesn't want to be left alone.

24   Jeff and Mandy hate the fighting. They don't know why their parents stay together when they fight that way. But the thought of one leaving is terrible too.

Besides being afraid that his parents will separate, Jeff is afraid that his father will kill his mother. Once Jeff stopped his father from hitting her with a fireplace poker. Jeff is afraid of what might happen when he isn't home. He worries that his little brother will get in his father's way. Living with his father's anger makes Jeff feel alone and different from other teens.

Loneliness

Keeping the "Don't Talk" rule makes Jeff, Mandy, and Larry feel alone. No one in the family talks about what's going on. They are alone in their home. They don't talk to people outside for fear of not being liked. Hiding their feelings, they feel all alone with their troubles. They think they are different from anyone else. They look the same, but they feel different inside.

Anger

Young people whose parents are chemically dependent live with their parents' anger. They also feel angry themselves.

The "Don't Talk" rule makes for a lonely life.

Jeff and Mandy hear yelling and screaming. Jeff fears that his father will hurt someone physically. Many homes are filled with terror of a parent who beats the children or the other parent. Doors are knocked down. Holes are kicked in walls. The children learn that being angry means being violent.

Mandy learned when she was little not to show anger. Her parents could scream and yell, but no one else could. She learned to hold her anger inside.

26   Anger held inside can cause stomach-aches, headaches, and other illnesses from stress. It makes teens act out the anger in other ways. Jeff gets into fights at school. He argues with teachers. He is always in trouble.

Holding her anger in keeps Mandy from doing her best in school. She just can't get moving. She feels bad about herself. She would like to talk about her feelings but is afraid to.

You need to let out your anger in ways that don't hurt you or anyone else. It's okay to be angry. Your parents aren't there for you when you need comfort. You hate their chemical use. You feel as though you live in a zoo. You hate feeling different because of them. Yes, you ARE angry. Now, take care of it.

- Talk to someone you trust.
- Go out in the garage, get in the car, roll up the windows, and scream.
- Pound your pillow with your fists. Hit it with a stick or bat.
- Go out and cuss at a tree.
- Start running every day.
- Join an aerobics class.
- Throw rocks in the river.
- Take the dog for a walk.
- Talk to someone you trust.

Think about what you're really angry about. It is the disease that makes your parents the way they are. It's the disease that is messing up your life. Get mad at the disease. That will help you see your parents differently. It will help you feel better about being in your family. The disease is causing you pain.

Guilt

Along with being angry, you wish the dependent parent were gone. Many teens wish the parent dead. Some think of ways to get rid of the parent. Then they feel guilty for having those feelings. It is natural to want to be rid of what causes you pain. You're not a bad person for having those feelings. You're human. You're like every other teenager who is living in an addicted family.

Young people often feel guilty about what is happening at home. Larry thought it was his fault that his mother didn't come home. He tried to do everything she wanted. No matter what he did, it wasn't the right thing. He felt guilty because he couldn't find the right thing to do.

You may feel guilty because your parents say it's your fault they drink. Maybe

28 | they call you names. Not being able to stop makes you feel guilty. Stop blaming yourself. Remember the 3 Cs: You didn't cause it. You can't control it. You can't cure it.

You must break the "Don't Talk, "Don't Trust," and "Don't Feel" rules. You have tried to hide the feelings, but you can't. Talk about your feelings to someone you trust.

Shame

When Mandy saw her father staggering down the street, she would cross to the other side. She was afraid that he might stop her, and someone might see. She was so ashamed of him.

Jeff did not bring his friends home. He didn't know how his father would act. Sometimes his father would be friendly. Other times he would criticize Jeff in front of his friends. Once he had even made fun of a friend's haircut. Jeff was so embarrassed that he quit having friends over. He hated feeling so ashamed.

If Larry's mother wasn't using speed, she was drinking. He tried to keep the house clean, but he couldn't. He was ashamed to have anyone see how he lived.

He learned to wash his clothes himself.
The nurse in elementary school first made
him know how dirty he was. She told him
to bathe every day. She helped him learn
to take care of himself. His mother never
seemed to notice if he was clean or not.
He still felt embarrassed and ashamed
about how dirty he used to be.

Feeling ashamed of parents and what
goes on in the house is the same for all
young people in chemically dependent
homes. The shame may grow to feeling
ashamed of yourself. Shame makes you
hate yourself. It makes you feel "dirty."
You feel not worthy of anyone's love. In
doing that, you have confused what your
parents do with who you are. You are not
your father or your mother. What they do
is not you. You need support from someone who understands your feelings.
Alateen groups have teens just like you.
Even if your parent abuses drugs other
than alcohol, Alateen groups will welcome
you. They understand the disease of
chemical dependence. They understand
how you feel. They have broken the "Don't
Talk" rule. You can find help and under-
standing with them.

When one parent is addicted the other is forced to deal with many problems alone.

CHAPTER 4

What's Going On with the Codependent Parent?

*T*he door slammed with a loud bang. Keith wished the house would fall down. "She's so unreasonable," he said to himself. He was all ready to go to the game when his mother decided she had to have a pound of coffee right now. Why couldn't she go after it herself? Sometimes Keith thinks she's crazy. Saturday he stayed home to help her around the house. All of a sudden she started yelling and said he was in the way. The week before she yelled at him for going out and leaving all the work for her. She's worse than his father, and she doesn't even drink.

Sandy leaned against the closed door of her bedroom and cried. She tried so hard to take care of the family. She did the grocery shopping and cooked dinner. She took care of the younger kids. She kept

32 the house as clean as she could. It wasn't her fault that Danny fell and broke his arm. Her father blamed her. He said she didn't care about anybody but herself. He said she should have watched Danny. Danny played next door all the time. She couldn't watch him every minute. Why didn't her mother take some responsibility for the kids? She tried to talk to her father about it. He said, "Well, your mother's very high-strung. Her nerves, you know." Sandy knew, all right. When something happened her mother grabbed her Valium and said, "Oh, my nerves!" Her "nerves" were an excuse to do nothing while Sandy did all the work. It was so unfair. And then for her father to be so mean to her. That hurt.

The Codependent Parent

A person affected by someone else's chemical dependence is called *codependent*. Codependents find ways to cope with what's happening in the family. They are always under stress. Joe, Sandy's father, took out his stress on the family. He said to Sandy all the things that he wanted to say to his wife. All the responsibility for the family falls on Joe. He gets no help in making decisions. He makes excuses for his wife to the rest of the family. He doesn't want anyone to come to the house. He doesn't see his friends anymore. He has no one to talk to. Joe is a lonely man, and he is very angry. The pressure builds, and he lets off steam. He feels guilty when he does it. As it happens more often Joe feels that something is terribly wrong with him. Chemical dependence is progressing in him too.

As the alcoholism of Keith's father gets worse, so does the codependence of his mother. She takes over more and more of her husband's responsibilities. When the water heater breaks, she calls the plumber. When the car needs tires, she gets them. Without her paycheck the bills couldn't be paid. She is worried about money all the time. She worries about what her husband is doing. She wonders where he is. She wonders how to make him stop drinking. She tries to keep others from finding out about it. She can't think straight any more. Keith thinks she's crazy sometimes, and so does she.

Worrying about the dependent makes the codependent neglect the family. One of the children takes over the job of parenting. Often the children feel the parents' neglect and take it out on each other.

34   At first, codependents make excuses for the dependent's behavior. They call in and say the person is sick when he's really hung over. They deny there's a problem. The codependent begins to get more and more angry. Then the nagging and fighting begin. If there is no fighting, the anger is there just the same. It is like living with a time bomb. Some homes are quiet and dead. Everyone is empty of feeling.

Living that way makes people behave strangely. Your codependent parents try very hard to control the drinking and what happens in the family. The harder they try, the worse things get. They feel very guilty because they can't control what goes on. Finally, they realize that they can't control themselves. They need help as much as the dependent.

You live in the same confusion, and you need help too. Learning to take care of yourself is very important. Alateen can help you do that. Your school counselor may have a list of places where you can get help. The school nurse often knows about groups in the community. Begin to look around for help. Talking about it with someone you can trust is your first step.

CHAPTER 5

How Do You Survive in All This?

*G*etting through the day in a chemically dependent home is a struggle. It's as though each person is playing a part in a mixed-up play. Roles are played out in the family.

Super-Good-Responsible

Karen thinks she must be perfect. She tries hard to do everything right. She takes care of the house and her younger brothers. Straight As and lots of school activities keep her very busy. Everyone thinks she's wonderful. Everyone but Karen. She sees only what she did not do well. She knows that if she *really* tried she could do much better. She never feels good enough. She's angry because she has to live in such a messed-up family. She's

35

36 angry about trying so hard and not getting any credit from her parents. Karen is acting the role of the Super-Good-Responsible kid.

Super-Bad-Irresponsible Troublemaker

Jerry has a brother like Karen. Jerry knows he can never be as good as Kevin. The only way Jerry ever got much attention was by being bad. He's as bad as his brother is good. Kevin tries hard, and Jerry doesn't try at all. Although Jerry acts as if he enjoys breaking the rules, inside he feels guilty for his bad behavior. He knows it's his fault, but he still feels rejected and lonely and hurt. He covers up all those feelings with anger. He's angry at his parents for not caring about him. He's angry with his father for using drugs. He's angry at Kevin for and getting all the attention. Most of all he's angry at himself for being such a screw-up. Jerry has taken on the role of Super-Bad-Irresponsible Troublemaker.

Flexible Adjuster

When you live in a world you can't count on, don't count on anything. That was Holly's motto. She could adjust to any situation. Nothing seemed to bother her.

The Super-Good-Responsible kid tries to do it all.

You have to be a Flexible Adjuster when your mother lies down on the job.

She just went along with what came down and didn't worry about it. But inside she was angry. Never having anyone to depend on made her angry. Not being able to count on anything made her angry. She was angry about living with a mother who was never there for her. Her mother might have been in the house, but she wasn't there for Holly. To survive in her family, Holly became a Flexible Adjuster.

Comedian

Kelly couldn't stand the tension in his house. When he was small, he didn't know what was going on. When he asked about his parents' fights, everyone would tell him there was no fight. He was mixed up and scared. Doing something funny always made everyone feel better—even Kelly. Today Kelly still uses laughter and joking to cover his feelings of confusion and fear. He is angry about what goes on in his house. But he still keeps the comedy going. His role is to break the tension in the family. He's the Comedian.

Invisible Loner

Lori got lost in the confusion of the family. She didn't like what was going on. She found out very young that taking care of herself was her best bet. She played by herself for hours. She stayed out of the way of the family. Today Lori still takes care of herself. She has little to do with the rest of the family. She doesn't know how to make friends at school. She feels lonely and different. No one pays attention to her, so she feels unimportant and worthless. Lori's role is to be an Invisible Loner.

Many teenagers in chemically dependent homes fit these roles. Some see themselves in two of the roles. You don't have to stay locked in a role. You can get help to deal with your feelings. Break the "Don't Talk" rule. Let others help you.

When your home is full of violence, the anger may rub off on you.

CHAPTER 6

It's a Violent and Terrifying Place

*T*he pounding of her heart was so loud
that Michelle was sure it could be heard at
the other end of the phone. She wanted to
hang up. If it were only herslf, she would.
But it was the little kids. She didn't want
them hurt. She didn't know what to do
about them. Michelle said into the phone,
"My father is an alcoholic. I'm afraid he's
going to hurt one of us real bad. Can you
help me?" The woman on the Teen Hot-
line set a time for Michelle to talk to a
counselor. After talking to the counselor
at the Center for Child Abuse Prevention,
Michelle had a safety plan.

41

42 | *What You Can Do*

If you live with violence in your home, here are some ideas for a safety plan.

- Find a safe place to go. A relative may agree to take you in when your parent is likely to abuse you. A friend can be your "port in a storm." Your town may have a shelter for victims of violence.
- Leave the house when the abusive parent is angry.
- Never argue with an angry parent.
- When accused or unjustly criticized, say nothing.
- Have a list of phone numbers of people and agencies that can help you.
- If you fear for the safety of anyone in the house, CALL THE POLICE. Don't worry about what anyone will think. Be safe.
- Talk to someone you trust.

Your parent does not have to beat you to be abusing you. Child abuse can include being locked in a closet, made to sit in one place for hours, deprived of food, called bad names or threatened, locked alone in a car, and left alone in the house. Neglect is another form of abuse. You are not cared for or provided for. Children who are not fed regularly, or not given proper health care are neglected.

There are people to help your family. **43** School counselors often know agencies where your family can be helped. County Health Departments have child protective services. The National Council on Alcoholism can help you or tell you where to get help. Their number is in the white pages of the telephone book. You deserve to be cared for physically and emotionally.

Sexual Abuse

The biggest secret in a chemically dependent family is sexual abuse. You may be a victim of sexual abuse without knowing it. Everyone knows that sexual intercourse is abuse. But there are other forms of sexual abuse.

Sharon hated to come home because her father made her sit in his lap. He'd put his hands all over her and feel her breasts.

Carl tried to be out when his Aunt Hazel visited. She gave him wet kisses on the mouth. It made him feel dirty.

Sue's uncle would stand at the end of the hall and unzip his pants and tell her he had something special to show her.

Jim's mother left her door open and stood naked where he could see her.

44   Carol's stepbrother walked close to her and put his hand on her bottom. He'd say, "You have a nice butt."

Jean's father told her to undress while he watched.

When Pam's stepfather called home and she answered the phone, he always said something about her body.

All of these young people were sexually abused.

No one has the right to touch your body if you don't want to be touched. No one has the right to touch you in a way you don't like. No one has the right to expose sexual parts to you. No one has the right to make you expose yourself. No one has the right to say things that make you feel uncomfortable. No one has the right to use you for sexual pleasure.

It's important for you to know that you are not to blame for what has happened to you. The adult is responsible for betraying your trust. Many agencies can help you. Look in the government section of your telephone book for mental health sevices. Sons and Daughters United is a group of people who were sexually abused. They meet in cities all over the country. You are not alone. There is help for you.

CHAPTER 7

Dealing with Your Dependent Parent

*T*ed looked at the paper Jill handed him. It was the list of Dos and Don'ts for coping with a chemically dependent parent. Every group member had brought ideas to go on the list. They met once a week with Mr. Oakwood, a special counselor for kids having problems with drugs. Ted and Jill are part of a group for students whose parents are alcoholic or doing drugs. They all need help dealing with their parents. After they have discussed today's list, they'll make a final list. They get lots of support from each other in group. Now they will have something to remind them of the things they talk about in group.

45

Managing the Unmanageable

46

You're well aware of the 3 Cs now. Don't think you're a helpless victim of the disease. You're a victim, but you're not helpless. There are things you can do to make your life at home more bearable. There are other things that are best not to do. Some of them may be very hard to do or to stop doing. You've done lots of hard things already. You can do this. It helps to have a support system like Ted and Jill's. Even one other person is helpful. Having someone you trust to share with helps you get through the hard times.

Things to Stop Doing

• *Don't blame.* Stop blaming your parents for drinking or doing drugs. Stop blaming them for everything that goes wrong. Stop blaming yourself for your parents' drinking or drug use. Stop blaming yourself for everything that goes wrong in the house. Blaming keeps everyone helpless. Nothing good happens when you blame.

• *Don't take things personally.* When your parents yell at you, it's the disease talking. Your parents hurt too. Get mad at the disease, not them.

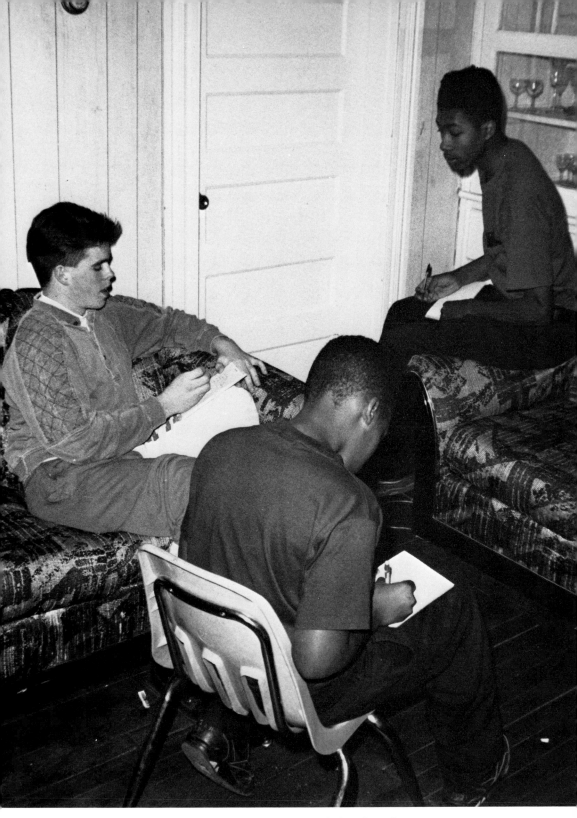

Meeting with peers in a support group can help when things are hard at home.

48

• *Don't cover for your parents.* Don't make excuses. Don't lie for them. Don't call the boss and say they're sick. Don't drag your father into the house when he passes out on the lawn. Don't put your mother to bed when she's too drunk to do it herself. Covering makes it easier for them to keep using drugs.

• *Don't try to control the drug use.* Getting rid of the supply won't help. They'll just get more. Don't ask them to promise not to drink or use. Don't look for them and try to bring them home. Their drug use can't be controlled until they get help.

• *Don't withdraw from others.* As the chemical dependence gets worse in your home, you may not want to be around others. You feel no one will like you because of your parents. You need to be with people. You need your friends to help you get your mind off your troubles. You need to talk to someone you trust. Don't let the disease make you a prisoner.

• *Don't try to talk to your parents when they've been drinking or using.* They're out of their minds then. You'd be talking to a chemical, not a person.

• *Don't feel ashamed and try to cover it up.* Don't tell lies about how wonderful everything is in your family. Don't laugh and pretend it's funny. *You are not your parents. Your parents are not you.* Nothing is wrong with you. Be proud of YOU.

• *Don't ride with a parent who has been drinking or using.* Your parent may be angry if you won't get in the car. That's okay. *You'll stay alive.*

• *Don't drink or use drugs yourself.* You see your parents try to escape their problems by drinking and using. You may want to use drugs to solve your problems too. DON'T. Your chances of becoming chemically dependent are too high.

Things to Do

• *Treat your parents with dignity and respect.* You may think they don't deserve it. If you yell at your parents, you won't feel good about *you.* You deserve to treat yourself better. Treat your parents as close friends who are visiting.

• *Go to Alateen or other support groups.* You need all the help you can get. In Alateen you'll find other teens who understand. Look in the white pages of the phone book for AlAnon. Ask them about Alateen.

• *Have outside interests.* Get your mind off what is wrong and onto what is right. You deserve to be happy. The only one

50   who can make you happy is you. Take responsibility for doing things that are good for you. Get involved in activities that are healthy and fun.

• *Let your parents know you love them.* Chemically dependent parents hate themselves. They don't think they're lovable at all. They need to know you care. Tell them when you know they haven't been drinking or using.

• *Be sure you and your family are safe.* Have a plan for your safety. If a parent gets violent go to a safe place. If you feel uncomfortable going to a neighbor or a friend in the middle of the night, GO ANY-WAY. Being safe is the most important thing. Have two copies of a list of emergency phone numbers. Keep one with you, and leave one in a safe place at home. Include these numbers: a relative or friend who will come to help you, the fire department, the police, the children's center where you can stay, your doctor, and an ambulance service. If you are on the 911 system, that one number will put you in touch with all emergency services.

• *Learn all you can about chemical dependence.* The more you know about the disease, the more you'll understand yourself and your family.

• *Be good to yourself.* Your family
doesn't give you the support and love you
deserve. It's important that you learn to be
loving to yourself. You can learn to tell
yourself the positive things you need to
hear. You can be your own best friend.
Get up each morning, look at yourself in
the mirror, and say:

I am lovable.
I respect myself.
I am special.
I am a caring person.
I am worthwhile.
I'm okay today.
I deserve only good things.
I am happy with myself.
I deserve to be happy.
I am my best friend.
It's okay if I'm not perfect.
I am capable and confident.
I like myself.
It's okay to please myself.
I am important.
I feel good about myself.
I am a good person.
I am the best me I can be.

Your world has been a world of pain and
confusion. You may not live in a happy
family, but you can be a happy person.

Having someone you trust to talk with can ease even a bad situation.

CHAPTER 8

Where Do You Go from Here?

*E*ric feels like the parent in his family. His alcoholic mother takes no responsibility for the house or family. Their father left the family because of her alcoholism. Besides trying to stay at the top of his class at school, Eric takes responsibility for the family. His younger brother depends on him to be both parents. Looking at his mother passed out on the sofa disgusts Eric. He feels like her parent, too. He's tired of having to comfort her just as he does his brother. He's tired of being leaned on. He needs someone to lean on.

54 | *Growing Up Too Fast*

Young people in chemically dependent homes carry too much responsibility for anyone so young. You grow up fast. You take on adult roles. Like Eric, you miss out on being a teenager. You feel much older than your classmates. Life is serious business. There's no time for fun. Like Eric, you need someone to lean on. There are people to help you. There are adults and other teens who understand the conflict inside you. There are places to go to get support.

A Word to Those Who Have a Chemically Dependent Mother

Nine out of ten wives stay with alcoholic husbands. Only one in ten men stays with an alcoholic wife. A chemically dependent mother is much more embarrassing than a father who is dependent. Mothers are supposed to take care of their family. A mother who does drugs or gets drunk is especially blamed by society. That makes it harder for you. Remember, you are not your mother. It's not your fault that she's the way she is.

Your mother doesn't drink or use because she wants to. She can't stop the way she's behaving. She needs help too.

Drugs and the Law   55

Many parents are using illegal drugs.
Do you call the police? How do you
handle that? *Handle it very carefully.* It's
important that you know what will happen
to them. It's even more important to know
what will happen to *you*.

A decision to call the police is too big
for you to make alone. Talk to someone
before you do anything. You need to dis-
cuss why turning your parents in would be
good and why it would be bad. What
would happen if it got into the news?
Where would you go if they went to jail?
Are there younger children in the family?
What about them? Those are just a few of
the questions you need answered before
you make a decision.

When you talk to someone, it's safest to
talk on the telephone. You don't have to
give your name. A drug "crisis" line is a
good place to start. The person who answers should be able to help or to tell you
where to find help.

A school counselor or a counselor from
a county agency is a good source. In some
cases the counselor may have to report
what you tell him or her. Call on the
phone first without giving your name.
Talk about what's happening in your family.

56 If the counselor tells you that it wouldn't have to be reported, go in person to talk. If it would have to be reported, ask the counselor whom you could talk to safely.

Your safety is the most important thing.

If you're in danger, get help. That means calling the police if necessary. If you are not in danger, get some help with making your decision.

To Use Or Not to Use Chemicals

The greatest abusers of chemicals are children of abusers. You say you won't be like your parents. You say, "It'll never happen to me. I know better." There are millions of alcoholics and addicts in the world today who said that.

Holly drinks at parties. She says she can control it. Holly is sure she won't have a problem. Her attitude will make her deny the signs of a problem in the future.

Andy isn't sure he can stand up to *peer pressure*. He's twelve and has been offered marijuana. He said no, but he isn't sure he'll be able to say no forever.

Everyone knows Jenny's parents are alcoholic. Her friends were surprised when they saw her drinking at a party. Jenny was with Jim for the first time. She

didn't want him to think she wasn't cool.
She feels guilty about drinking.

Bill wants nothing to do with any drugs.
All of his uncles are alcoholic. His grand-
father died from alcoholism. His brother
is freaked out on crack. He's sure that he'll
become chemically dependent if he ever
gets close to alcohol or other drugs.

Holly, Andy, Jenny, and Bill will never
be "normal" chemical users. Their fears
and attitudes about alcohol and other
drugs put them in a class of their own. It's
best for all of them to stay away from alcohol and other drugs.

You know that you are at high risk for
chemical dependence if your parents are
chemically dependent. How can you tell if
you will be dependent yourself? You can't.
How can you be sure that you *won't* be
chemically dependent? Don't drink or use
other drugs.

Getting Help

Reading this book is a step toward help-
ing yourself. The HELP LIST that follows
has lots of places where you'll find people
who will give you a hand toward a happier
life. Reach out. You have nothing to lose
but your loneliness and pain.

Help List

Telephone Book
Yellow Pages
• Alcoholism, Drug Abuse, Counselors

Government Listings
• Alcoholsm Treatment, Drug Abuse, County Health Services, Child Protective Services

Associations
• National Association of Children of Alcoholics
31706 Pacific Coast Highway
South Laguna, CA 95677
(714) 499-3889

• National Council on Alcoholism
12 West 21st Street
New York, NY 10010
(212) 206-6770

• AlAnon Family Group Headquarters
P.O. Box 182, Madison Square Station
New York, NY 10159

• Narcotics Anonymous
World Service Office
16155 Wyandotte Street
Van Nuys, CA 91406

• Daughters and Sons United
P.O. Box 952
San Jose, CA 95108-0952

Hot Line 800-Cocaine
Answers any questions about cocaine.

Glossary
Explaining New Words

addiction Compulsion to use a drug, with loss of control and continued use no matter what happens to you or others.

AlAnon Community group of people who are affected by someone else's alcohol (and other drug) use and who meet to share feelings and help one another deal with problems.

Alateen Community group of young people who are affected by someone else's alcohol (and other drug) use and who meet to share feelings and help one another deal with problems.

Alcoholics Anonymous (AA) Community group of chemically dependent people who meet to share their feelings and help one another to stay well and not drink or use other drugs.

alcoholism Illness that causes people to become dependent on alcohol because of changes in the brain.

chemical dependence Strong feeling of need for a drug that causes people to

60 keep taking the drug even when it is harmful.

cocaine Powerful stimulant of the central nervous system taken from the leaves of the coca plant and made into a powder that is sniffed, smoked, or injected.

Cocaine Anonymous (CA) Community group of cocaine addicts who meet to share their feelings and help one another to stay well and not use cocaine or other drugs.

codependent Someone affected by another person's dependence on alcohol/ drugs.

compulsive Happening again and again; uncontrolled need to do something again and again.

denial Unwillingness to admit the truth; unwillingness to admit there is a problem with chemicals.

drug Chemical substance that changes how the mind or body works.

illegal Against the law.

peer Someone your own age.

prescription drugs Medicines that must be ordered by a doctor and prepared by a pharmacist.

speed Street name for amphetamines; also called uppers, pep pills, bennies, dexies, meth, crystal, crank.

For Further Reading

Easy to Read

Brooks, Cathleen. *The Secret Everyone Knows.* San Diego: Operation Cork, 1979.

Hornik, Edith. *You and Your Alcoholic Parent.* New York: Associated Press, 1974.

Seixas, Judith. *Living with a Parent Who Takes Drugs.* New York: Glenwillow Books, 1989.

Shuker, Nancy. *Everything You Need to Know about an Alcoholic Parent.* New York: Rosen Publishing Group, 1990.

Not as Easy to Read, But Worth the Effort

Cooney, Judith. *Coping with Sexual Abuse,* rev. ed. New York: Rosen Publishing Group, 1990.

Hornik-Beer, E.A. *A Teenager's Guide to Living with an Alcoholic Parent.* Center City, MN: Hazelden, 1984.

62 Kurland, Morton L. *Coping with Family Violence,* rev. ed. New York: Rosen Publishing Group, 1990.

Leite, Evelyn, and Espeland, Pamela. *Different Like Me: A Book for Teens Who Worry about Their Parents' Use of Alcohol/Drugs.* Minneapolis: Johnson Institute, 1987.

McFarland, Rhoda. *Coping with Substance Abuse,* rev. ed. New York: Rosen Publishing Group, 1990.

Newman, Susan. *It Won't Happen to Me.* New York: Putnam Publishing Group, 1987.

Porterfield, Kay Marie. *Coping with an Alcoholic Parent,* rev. ed. New York: Rosen Publishing Group, 1990.

Scott, Sharon. *How to Say No and Keep Your Friends.* Amherst, MA: Human Resource Development Press, 1986.

To Read to Younger Children

Berger, Gilda. *Making Up Your Mind about Drugs.* New York: Lodestar Books, 1988.

Black, Claudia. *My Dad Loves Me, My Dad Has a Disease.* Newport Beach, CA: ACT, 1979.

Index

About the Author

Rhoda McFarland has taught all grades, kindergarten through twelfth. She is a certified alcoholism and drug abuse counselor having worked with troubled young people and their parents. She developed and implemented the first educational program in the California area for students making the transition from drug/alcohol treatment programs back into the regular school system. She is currently working as a Peace Corp volunteer in Belize, Central America.

Photo Credits
Cover Photo: Chuck Peterson
Photos on pages 2, 8, 13, 17, 20, 25, 30, 37, 47, 52, Stuart Rabinowitz; page 40, Stephanie FitzGerald

Design & Production; Blackbirch Graphics, Inc.